Journey of

MIKE LEAGUE

ISBN 979-8-89130-012-5 (paperback)
ISBN 979-8-89130-013-2 (digital)

Christian Faith Publishing
832 Park Avenue
Meadville, PA 16335
www.christianfaithpublishing.com

Printed in the United States of America

Journey of Love

♡

As I consider the honor to write a foreword for a book that expresses the love between a husband and his bride, I am deeply humbled. The love shared in a marriage has the potential to move mountains far beyond what most of us ever experienced. Through the journey that Mike and Sandra lived, he learned to love her, serve her, and honor her up to her last breath. It is easy to overlook the gravity of the promise made to our spouse and God when we get married, but as Mike explains, Sandra's Heavenly Father would be watching to ensure she was well taken care of. While Sandra was fighting her battle, Mike had his own to fight. He lived the reality of Colossians 3:23–24, "Whatever you do, do your work heartily, as for the Lord rather than for men, knowing that from the Lord you will receive the reward of the inheritance. It is the Lord Christ whom you serve." Sandra was the best friend I could have imagined, and she fought the good fight. I can say with certainty that she had the freedom to continue pouring herself into others, which is what she did best because she felt loved beyond words by her husband. Mike was honest about the challenges he endured, but he chose "to put on love, which is the perfect bond of unity" (Colossians 3:14).

Janae Walsh

In a time when the world is asking the question, "What is love?" Journey of Love gives us a true glimpse into the reality of love lived out. I am forever marked and encouraged by Mike's transparency, vulnerability, and his story.

—Molly

*****

Mike, the creator of this book, is my uncle. In this book, you will find how the father's love was expressed through him to his wife, Sandra, through the journey of what was the most difficult time of both of their lives. It is a call to be exactly that. To be a reflection of the One who created us, to your loved one that may be going through a similar battle. I know it was not an easy task, but as he says in his writings, "for better or worse" means exactly that. How will you love or extend His love to those who are in the depths of it, is what I was left asking myself after reading this. His love never fails, and she was definitely surrounded by it!

—Michelle

*****

It was my wife's and my great pleasure to get to know Mike and Sandra. Mike's story is a great inspiration to me as a young husband who needs real Godly examples of a true gospel-like marriage. For me, it made me reflect back on my wedding day not so long ago. As I was standing in front of my beautiful bride making these vows before God, did I really understand "until death do us part" or "for better or worse"? Yes, the words were coming out of my mouth, but did I understand the severity of this covenant I was making before God? I kid myself and say I understood them, but I'm not so sure I really did until I read Mike's journey with Sandra and what he endured behind closed doors. I would see Mike almost every day, and I knew things were hard, but I did not know half of it. Despite everything he was going through, he would give me a friendly wave or walk over and talk to me about a project. It was hard for me to ask about Sandra a lot, but I just assured Mike we were praying, and Mike would smile and say I knew and that everything was going to be ok. Mike would share a few things with me about knowing who your friends were when times got hard, but we didn't help them because we felt sorry for them. We helped them because it's what God commanded us to do, and it just felt like they were an extended part of our family. We don't understand why Sandra's story ended the way it did, but I know beyond a shadow of a doubt God is using this story to touch so many people's life. I think that every couple who is thinking about marriage or is married would benefit greatly from hearing this story. It's so sweet to see the message of a savior who died for us being lived out in a marriage where a husband stayed with his wife until the end. He gave up his wants and needs as a man and put hers first, loved her no matter what. I believe Mike always saw Sandra just like he did on their wedding day, just as beautiful as ever with God in the middle. Mike, thank you for being a real man who can show us younger ones just how serious our words on that day mean. God has great things for you, and I look forward to walking with you in your ministry.

—Steven Lumbley

This is my attempt to put down on paper my experiences and the lessons that I learned while engaged in a battle with my wife with her cancer diagnosis and subsequent treatment. This would prove to be a very tough battle for me and my family.

If I recall correctly, she got her diagnosis in about April or May of 2020. At the time of this diagnosis, we had been married for twenty-three years. We were a blended family, and I had three kids from a previous marriage, and she had one child whom I later adopted. It is my utmost desire that if and when someone reads this or shares it with someone else, they receive a blessing and hopefully a strong reminder about the promise we all make to our spouses when we say our vows to each other at our wedding. I will say to anyone reading this that I hope you never have to go through this battle. It was a very tough and life-changing journey for me personally and for our kids. At this point in time of writing this, it's been almost a year since my best friend, ally, and companion rose up out of this life into eternity to be with her Father.

I want to start by asking a question. When you said your vows to each other at your wedding, were you serious, or had you ever even given them much thought, or were they just part of what you had to do to get through this part of the new journey with one another? Do you believe that when you did say those vows before God and family from that point on, you had a heavy responsibility to each other? About a week before I started writing this, I met a lady at a home improvement store who had survived the same type of cancer my wife had. In her battle, she told me her husband helped her very little. She is one of the reasons I decided to write this. Now anyone who is married knows there's a lot of work and effort to maintain and enjoy a good relationship with your spouse. It is really both of you who decide to be all in all the time to make it work.

I am going to speak on the part of our vows that most of us, I'm sure all, say as part of the wedding ceremony, "For better or for worse, in sickness and in health, till death do us part." I will say that Sandra and I grew a lot in our twenty-five years together. This was both of our second marriages. We both learned a lot along this journey about loving each other and being a team. It was the combined result of these lessons learned that prepared us for the battle looming ahead of us. We gain strength and wisdom along the way that prepares us for the next struggle facing us, and we learn to make wiser decisions for the betterment of each other.

My goal in writing this is to inspire you, the reader, to love your spouses, families, and friends on a much deeper level than you ever thought possible. It is not too late to change if you recognize the fact that any changes need to be made. Remember, we often don't get to choose our battles. We do, however, get to choose how we respond to them when they come. So hold on, read on, and if need be, make some changes. Tomorrow is not promised for any of us. Live today to the fullest.

When Sandra first received her diagnosis, I heard God speak to me, and He told me this: "This is my daughter. I'm watching you, so take good care of her."

This was my chance to show God, Sandra, our kids, and whoever else was watching that I understood my promise to her that I made at our wedding twenty-five years earlier. I was now about to really walk this out. This was the hardest thing I have ever done.

Think back to a time when your spouse or one of your kids maybe were sick. Only you really know the answer, but how did you handle it? Was it an inconvenience of your time? Were you angry for the inconvenience of it all? Maybe it interrupted some plans y'all made together, a vacation, a holiday trip, or maybe just the cost of it all? I must say that I've been there. I own that T-shirt. I also knew that for me, at this point, that line of thinking was not an option. My wife needed me, and she needed me at my best, and it was the best I was going to give her. Nothing short of that was gonna work, and I still had no idea at this point how far I was going to have to go to walk this out. Over this next two years battle, I was going to be stretched and pulled and called upon like never before.

Sandra was a researcher. She was a student of learning things she could use to help others. She was always trying to help those she loved and cared about to feel better. To be healthier, she studied the body and nutrition and was a massage therapist and she gave her all to that end for lots of people. When she received her diagnosis, she had already been researching cancer so she would know better how to help some of her patients who had cancer. She really wanted to help them the best she could. This also proved to be a very good thing because when she received her diagnosis, she almost immediately knew the treatment plan she would follow. She didn't have to cram it all in after the fact and make decisions in haste and in fear.

My job at this point was to love and support her in her decisions and to start taking up any slack I could in order to help her in her daily life during this time. I had to give her the time and space to fully focus on her treatment. My first item to take care of was to rearrange my responsibilities. Not only was I working a full-time job, but I had to start taking on as many of the daily routine things that are part of running a household as I could in order to free her time up so she could stay focused and make her life easier. I was already doing a large portion of the laundry and most of the cooking (I like to cook), but I started looking for ways to jump in and do more where I could when I could.

The next change I would make would be a huge change for me. I knew Sandra was going to be making some changes to her diet. She was always doing her research, and from all her reading, she was learning that certain foods feed cancer and other foods help fight it. So the diet path she was going to be on was a different path from that we were currently on. I was now going to be learning how to prepare more of a Mediterranean-style diet for us. The big change for us here was that we ate quite a bit of BBQ. I was in the barbecue competition scene, and to be good, I had to practice. It was not uncommon at all for us to be eating BBQ on most weekends as we tried out the latest recipe tweaks. This was some good family times with the kids and friends. We all loved bar barbecue. At some point during this, Sandra got some DNA test results back from a test she had taken. She had a gene malfunction/mutation which prevented the body from recognizing cancer cells and, therefore, could not tell the body to fight it. Come to find out, one of the causes of this malfunction was the eating of a lot of smoked meats. This was devastating news for me. I now had to deal with the question was I the reason my wife had cancer? The aftermath of that news was no more BBQ. I knew I couldn't make it and expect her not to want any, so I did the loving thing and sold my competition pit and quit making BBQ. If you are not sure of the difference, let me settle it for you now. Brisket, ribs, chicken, and pork butt are much better than what I was about to prepare and eat. I could always stop and get something for myself on the way home and eat it, which I did sometimes.

Another big change for me was sweets. We both liked them, and I knew I couldn't plop beside her and ask her questions while enjoying a Little Debbie. Little Debbie and I used to be very close. I had to focus on and support Sandra in this battle and was willing to make these changes for her, for us.

During this time, Sandra's main focus was on research and taking notes. She still had her friends, and they all spent time with her, which she enjoyed. Sandra was a great friend to have.

The thing about her that I miss the most now is her being there when I come home from work. This was always a big deal for her, and she always took her time to look her best for me. She wanted to spend time with me and hear about my day. She made that part of each workday a special event. After twenty-five years of having that, it is now a very quiet time for me when I go home. She loved spending that time with her Mikey.

Her friends also learned this about her. She was an expert at making the friend she was spending time with feel like they were loved, valued, and appreciated. She knew how to ask questions, and she asked many of them to draw things out of the person she was talking to. I also learned to share time with her with others.

At this point, we had been on this journey for about a year. So far, during this time period, she was still highly functional. She was still able to drive, and she truly loved to zip around in her car. She still did some shopping and ran errands to get a break from her research and routine. She had quite a few doctor appointments to make during this time and was able to drive to these herself.

At this point, this is also when I really started to take over almost entirely all the household duties. I still had a full-time job but was now doing the laundry, learning how to do the online bill paying, grocery shopping, doing the yard work, and doing or fixing whatever else popped up. This became my new normal, and I knew Sandra needed my help, and I was willing to do whatever it took to make her life easier. I truly loved my wife. She was worth it. She never saw or heard me complain. I was doing my utmost to be supportive and positive for her. I also knew she would be doing the same for me if the situation were reversed. For me, this was an honor and a pleasure, not an inconvenience.

Somewhere during this time, she could no longer get comfortable sleeping in our bed and moved to the couch. So I moved to the recliner beside her.

It was also around this time that subtle changes were starting to show in her that she was struggling. She was starting to struggle physically and mentally. This was a rough time for all of us. Our kids were a huge blessing along this journey as well as her friends. Sandra never wavered in her belief that she was going to be healed and walk away from this and be a living testimony of God's goodness and power. I would have gladly swapped places with her if I could have. I personally never asked God the why question. I guess I just figured He was much bigger than I would ever know, and I didn't feel qualified to question Him about anything. To this day, I haven't asked Him why it happened, but what I was asking Him was to show me how to make the changes in my life now in order to be more help and support for her and to honor her when she really needed it the most.

The people where I worked were very supportive, and the boss gave me the freedom to take some time off when I needed to in order to facilitate doctor visits and on the hard days for her. At this point in the battle, for me, any little bit helped. She still had her friends also that came over when they could to pray with her and encourage her.

It's hard to describe what I was feeling at this point in the journey other than just saying I was being stretched. I think most of the time, I was learning to a greater degree, how to think on my feet. I had a lot on my plate, and there seemed like insufficient time to figure some things out, so I had to hone my quick-thinking skills. Thank God for family and friends who were willing to jump in and help do anything.

From the one-year point to the eighteen-month point in this journey is when the biggest signs of the battles tole became more obvious. It was obvious the cancer was progressing, and the struggle for Sandra was becoming much harder. It was becoming harder for everyone involved in it with us. Cancer is not a one-person struggle. For me, it was very hard to watch my soulmate decline the way she was. This, I believe, was the hardest thing I've ever had to deal with.

I believe now would be a good time to address the most asked question to me during this journey.

How are you doing? This question was one I came to dislike very much for several reasons:

1. I don't have the time to adequately relay to you how I'm doing. I'm busy.
2. I don't believe the people asking the question really have the time, nor are they really prepared to hear the full explanation.
3. I do, however, understand why people ask the question, and I've asked it myself many times. It's a safe question to ask. It requires zero response from the person asking the question.

Here is what I believe would be the appropriate question. How can I help? Where are your cleaning supplies? Give me a grocery list, and let me go do that for you. Can I take a two-hour shift here at the house so you can get some free time or time to pray, think, scream, or cry. The struggle is real. I'm just saying if you really want to help, just look around sometimes. Assess the situation and be willing to insert yourself into the chaos and make a difference. It will be most appreciated by those in the struggle.

I think I felt like, for the most part, I was just going from fire to fire most times, so *any* help was a huge blessing, and we did have it. When you are in a position like this, it really shows you where your heart is at.

I think it's easy for most people when it's easy, but the tough times often bring out the bad inside of people. It would be easy for some in our situation to say that they didn't sign up for this and check out. This could be a bad marriage, bad health, or any number of reasons that causes some to give up. Love doesn't run, and it doesn't give up. This was the promise we made to each other.

For better or for worse, in sickness and in health, till death do us part.

For my family, it is now Christmastime in 2021. We are eighteen months into this journey. We all met at my son's house this year—our four kids, their spouses and kids, and my sister and her husband. We all had a wonderful time together, and I know we all enjoyed watching Sandra have fun. She was in good spirits on this occasion. This would be the last gathering we all had with her while she was fully functioning and having a blast. She was still believing in her miracle and was still glad to be alive and able to fight. That changed quickly for her after the time we had with her.

This was the time when I was most grateful for family and friends who were there in the battle with us. Even Moses, at one point, had to have two of his friends hold up his arms so he could pray so Israel would be victorious in a battle. I didn't have big faith prayers to pray. I was in the trenches and worn-out from doing everything necessary to keep things going. Others were praying the big prayers while I was fighting a battle.

Sandra really started going downhill quickly at this point. From this point on, she needed help with just about everything she did. I remember telling my daughter Briana after the first time I had to help her with her bathroom duties that it just got real. Yes, it just got real. I never forgot what God had told me up front. This is my daughter, and I'm watching you.

This, for me, was also the complete takeover of every aspect of keeping a house running. I did have some help, but all the weight was on my shoulders. I developed a deeper love and appreciation for my family, I think, at this point. My wife's friends became more like angels than friends.

Sometime around the first of April, Sandra had two back-to-back seizures. I saw both of these. I wouldn't wish that on anybody. That was one of the things I believe I could say traumatized me. It was scary. The other sad thing at this time was that she pretty much turned on me. I know now that it is not uncommon for people in her position to turn on those they are closest to. That would be me.

While we were at the hospital because of the seizures is when my family and I found out that the cancer was now in four spots on her brain also. We knew it had spread to her lungs and liver, and I also later found out it was in her stomach as well. She had kept this a secret from us. While in the hospital, I contacted her mom, and she came down from Dallas and moved in with us. This lady was a Godsend. To see Sandra like this was very tough. Even though she didn't like me, I was very glad for every minute I had with her. Sandra and her mom became best friends. It was good to see her happy. I would have an occasional good moment with her, and that would keep me going.

After she came home from the hospital, every time someone came to see her, she would not let them leave until she prayed for them and blessed them. Here she was, fighting for her life and still giving of herself to others. This was truly amazing to watch. As hard as all this was to watch, I felt it was an honor to be her husband and her best friend. She was, at this point, down to about ninety pounds.

My daughter and I got the sense that she was waiting on some event to take place before she loosened her grip on this life. The day came when she had her mom, her two brothers, and me all under one roof. They all had a good time together and a time of reconciliation before they left. It was a joy to watch.

Shortly after this, I was with Sandra, and I believe it was in the morning. I do not remember what was said, but I do remember her beautiful smile that I had not seen in some time directed at me. For me at that moment, I just won the grand prize. I knew she knew who

I was, and at that moment, she was glad to see me. That was the last time I saw that smile.

I believe it was the next day that she slipped from this life into eternity. I was there with her when she passed. It was on June 15 at about 2:00 a.m. when she shook off her cancer and left.

It is now May 12 as I'm writing this. Just about one month shy of a year since she left us for her celebration. How am I doing? Well, I've slowed down, way down. I left my full-time job and now work part-time. I want to spend as much time as I can with my family and enjoy them. I sold our house and gave almost everything we had accumulated in our twenty-five years of marriage away. I blessed as many as I could. I gave her car to a single mom in need. I bought an RV and moved into an RV park, and I absolutely love it. I have a group of neighbors who have the most well-behaved, respectful kids I have ever been around. This group of friends has taken me in and has shown me the love I needed to get through to the end of this journey. I also am still very lonely after having a great companion for so many years. It's very quiet when I'm home alone. Sandra and I laughed a lot together and became extremely close. I now have the freedom to go and do whatever I want when I want but still find it to be a most difficult decision sometimes just to decide what restaurant to eat at. Nothing is the same.

I recently had a conversation with two of my neighbor ladies about love. It was about the difference between being loving versus being love, two different things. In writing this, after that conversation, I was reminded of a truth I heard years ago. YOU CAN GIVE WITHOUT LOVING, BUT YOU CANNOT LOVE WITHOUT GIVING. I guess I've realized that I could not have or would not have gone through this battle with Sandra to the end as a loving person. I went through it as a man who had learned to love his wife and became love for her. When she couldn't stand, I held her up. When she couldn't walk, I walked for her. When she couldn't wipe her butt anymore, I wiped it for her. The first time I did this, by the way, was very awkward.

When I had wiped her backside, she chuckled and said, "You're not done. You still have to wipe the front."

When she couldn't love me back, I kept on loving her. I have no regrets, personally. I'm writing this to tell you I did everything possible as a man, as a friend, and as a husband to get my wife through this battle. My job was to get her across the finish line. I know this for sure, without a doubt. When she crossed that finish line, she got her reward. Mine was in knowing that at that moment, God was smiling at me and saying Mike League, job well done, son.

I still miss her like crazy. This is my new encouragement for almost everybody I speak to now. Make every second count with those you love. Tomorrow is not promised. Life has a new meaning for me now. I enjoy time with my kids and grandkids like never before. Every day is truly a gift. I'm always looking for ways to look outward to others. To help someone else make it. Our lives are to be lived to make a difference. Make it count.

One final side note, my son is learning to BBQ. Our first competition, together with me helping him, he got fifth place in chicken. The following week, I entered another one with a friend of mine, and we got first place in chicken and fourth in pork. Good friends, good barbecue, and a great cup of coffee go a long way.

About the Author

The author is a sixty-one-year-old man who lost his wife to triple-negative breast cancer on June 2022. In the following pages, you will read about a portion of their two-year battle with this cancer.

It is the desire of the author that this message reaches the right person or the right people. His story will help and encourage those struggling in their marriage through sickness or a spouse's or partner's sickness. This is his story of love, commitment, and determination to help his wife through her journey and battle with cancer.

He is simply a man who took his commitment seriously and let God do the rest. His hope is that you are more equipped and more blessed on your next journey.